IMAGES
of America

DUDE RANCHING
IN ARIZONA

IMAGES
of America

DUDE RANCHING
IN ARIZONA

Russell True
Foreword by Diana Madaras

ARCADIA
PUBLISHING

Published by Arcadia Publishing
Charleston, South Carolina

Printed in the United States of America

Library of Congress Control Number: 2016941967

For all general information, please contact Arcadia Publishing:
Telephone 843-853-2070
Fax 843-853-0044
E-mail sales@arcadiapublishing.com
For customer service and orders:
Toll-Free 1-888-313-2665

Visit us on the Internet at www.arcadiapublishing.com

To all the dude ranchers past, present, and future,
because as they uniquely know, there truly is nothing else like it.
And to all the guests who make it possible.

CONTENTS

FOREWORD

The romance of the authentic West is alive and well and accessible, all thanks to America's dude ranches. I am an artist who needs an occasional escape from the frantic pace, and I find restoration, peace, and inspiration on my annual treks to White Stallion Ranch just outside of Tucson, Arizona. The cowboy guitarist sings by the evening campfire, wranglers flip flapjacks in the desert during the morning breakfast ride, guests on horseback squeal with delight as they learn to herd calves into the pens, and they fly like the wind on fast rides to the mountain pass. To breathe in the creosote-sweetened air, gaze upon the sprawling open range, and commune with the horse beneath me who ambles so sure-footedly along the trail—that is my dude ranch experience.

Hats off to all the dude ranchers across the country for doing the backbreaking work required to keep the ranches going and resisting the temptation to sell out to developers. I thank God for the preservation of the magnificent tract of land that is White Stallion Ranch every time I cross its threshold. And many thanks to Russell True for undertaking the monumental task of compiling this book that helps preserve the rich history of Arizona's dude ranches. They are an important portal into the past, a living lesson in history and tradition that is the American cowboy and the American West. How lucky are we to be able to experience our rich heritage in real time?

—Diana Madaras

ACKNOWLEDGMENTS

For a lifetime dude rancher, finding great old photographs, doing the research, and discovering ranches unknown to me was almost a pilgrimage. Growing up in the 1960s and 1970s, I knew or knew of many of the ranches and ranchers, especially in the Tucson area. Revisiting them was nostalgic and fun. Going back to the early days of dude ranching in Arizona through the glory years of the 1940s and 1950s was fascinating.

All this was the fun part. Without my wife, Laura, who typed every handwritten caption and, over and over again, showed me how to use technology and then did it for me anyway, this book would not have happened. Her mother, Chris Holden, put her experience teaching English literature to work editing and cleaning up all that needed her help.

My friend Ian Singer pursued leads, conducted research, and bird-dogged the ranchers for their photographs and history. Dude ranchers are overworked, underpaid, and spend a lot of their time "putting out fires." Despite their good intentions, not much happened while their ranches were in season. Ian never gave up.

Susanne Walsh, who spent years in Wickenburg and worked at ranches there, was invaluable in putting together that chapter. Thanks to her knowledge, contacts, and the incredible Desert Caballeros Western Museum, that chapter came together the easiest.

Jaye Wells helped immeasurably by researching dude ranching and the photography at the Arizona Historical Society in Tucson. His artistic eye, interest in history, and contacts from the very helpful AZHS were significant to compiling the Tucson chapter.

Of course, a giant thank-you is due to all the owners and managers who pulled the photographs off the walls, dug the files out of the basements, and pulled the albums from the shelves, all to be part of this book. They provided the historical background and double-checked the facts. In short, thanks go to the huge number of people who contributed to make *Dude Ranching in Arizona* possible.

INTRODUCTION

Dude ranching in Arizona has a far richer and more important role in history than most know. This is true both for its place in the dude-ranching industry overall and for its early importance to tourism in the state. Dude ranching did not start in Arizona. The idea of tourists staying as guests on ranches, or in the rural West, likely started independently in a few places. Now, it is generally acknowledged that the birthplace was the Eaton brothers' Custer Trail Ranch in the Dakota Territory, founded in 1882. They moved their operation to Wyoming in 1903 and simply called it Eaton's Ranch. The Eaton family also owned and operated the Rimrock Ranch, near the town of the same name, in Arizona for several years. Other well-known dude ranchers from the North tried dude ranching in Arizona. Legendary founding president of the Dude Ranchers' Association, Larry Larom took his Valley Ranch School for Boys to the Saguaro Lake Ranch in 1934 and encouraged his dude ranch guests to go to Kay El Bar Ranch for the 1936 winter season. The Van Cleves of Montana founded Lazy K Bar Ranch outside of Tucson, and the Millers converted a closed boys school into Elkhorn Ranch (South).

In Arizona, Wickenburg is probably where the first dude ranches opened. The idea quickly spread, with the majority of the ranches located in the southern half of the state. Tucson and Wickenburg both laid claim to the title "Dude Ranch Capital of the World" at different times. If the total number of ranches is the criteria, Tucson probably had the most during the 1940s and 1950s. In his 1976 University of Arizona master's thesis, Frank Blaine Norris lists 107 total ranches in the Tucson area, with several changing names, styles, and identities over time. In 1950, there were about 50 ranches in Tucson and 100 in Southern Arizona. At the time, the ranches brought in an estimated $10 million annually to the area. Though smaller in number, Wickenburg had a thriving dude ranch community. Given the smaller size of the town compared to Tucson, dude ranching likely had an even larger impact there.

Dude ranching has always had many challenges, several of which are unique to the industry. The dude ranch experience is built on expansive, unspoiled, beautiful country, along with extensive and varied horseback riding. The ranches near the bigger cities like Phoenix, Tucson, and, to a lesser extent, Wickenburg were often swallowed up by the explosive growth of these towns. Housing developments, malls, office complexes, and so on stand where dudes once rode horses.

Most ranches were small, with an average guest capacity of 35–40. The majority were seasonal. Despite their small size, many ranches had several amenities, such as swimming pools, tennis courts, hot tubs, game rooms, and more. Nearly all of them served three meals daily. To survive, the ranches needed to stay fairly full.

While the more rural ranches were less burdened by the threat of urban growth, they suffered from a lack of proximity to railroad stations and airports, which often made staffing more difficult. Recessions are hard on ranches, and any dip in the number of dudes hits a business hard that has horses who need to eat and a staff who generally lives on the ranch. The positive to all this is that dude ranching will remain a business only for those owners and managers who believe in the unique and special experience that they share with their guests.

One

WICKENBURG AREA RANCHES

In 1862, German-born Henry Wickenburg joined the Pauline Weaver party to prospect in the valley along Hassayampa Creek. In October of the following year, Wickenburg discovered a quartz ledge that he believed had potential. He filed a claim along with his associates and began to work the mine alone, establishing a nearby encampment called Wickenburg Ranch. Soon, a town sprang up with stamp mills, stores, saloons, and hotels. It was simply called Wickenburg. Henry Wickenburg's Vulture Mine ultimately produced $70 million worth of gold, which solidified its position as the most important gold mine in Arizona.

Henry Wickenburg had several homes in the area. His first along the Hassayampa River was located on the 1,600-acre Bar FX Ranch. The owner Mary O'Brien remodeled and redecorated the home and used it for parties and events. The most popular aspect of the house was the tunnel under the floor that Wickenburg had built to escape from the Apaches.

The Wickenburg area is likely where dude ranching began in Arizona. Though several other ranches claim the honor, the Garden of Allah was almost certainly the first dude ranch in the state. Several Ranches followed, and as soon as the early 1930s, Wickenburg was claiming the title of "Dude Ranch Capital of the World." Tucson, Phoenix, and Rimrock followed with their own concentrations of ranches.

With easy access to Phoenix by railroad or highway, Wickenburg was a terrific location for dude ranching. It was also a small, scenic town that retained its history and character as a tight-knit community of dude ranchers, with several owners shifting locations, partnerships that came and went, ranches with multiple names, and many that opened and closed or were reborn as something different.

The Garden of Allah was likely the first dude ranch in Arizona. The ranch started out as a stage stop in 1860, and the building, which also included lodging, is still in use. In 1912, Alaska gold prospector Dr. John Sanger, along with a partner named Chapman, bought the 960 acres of the Brill Ranch that included the stage stop, and there, they opened the Garden of Allah. All guests were welcome except those with infections or contagious diseases. This rule was designed to exclude those with tuberculosis since so many people with the disease came to Arizona for the dry air. There were 26 flowing springs on the property, allowing the ranch to grow its own alfalfa. Eight guest cottages lined the 500-foot-long natural swimming area in one of the small streams. Guests from Phoenix often came to enjoy the cooler temperatures along the river. The Garden of Allah had its own railroad stop. Dr. Sanger disappeared in 1915, and his partner Chapman was unable to continue the operation, thus the ranch was sold and closed in 1916. The man in this photograph is unidentified. (Courtesy of Desert Caballeros Western Museum.)

In 1925, Leo and Nell Weaver reopened the Garden of Allah under the name Circle Flying W Ranch. As with many ranches, the brand became the name. The ranch brand is easy to see on the surrey in this photograph. Wickenburg's first golf course was built on the Circle Flying W. The ranch was also known for its modern stable, which drew many polo ponies and the highest-jumping horse in the Southwest, Prince Daring. (Courtesy of Desert Caballeros Western Museum.)

In 1930, Leb Chapman purchased the Circle Flying W and renamed it the Lazy RC Ranch. This was the same ranch that began as the 1860 stage stop and took guests in 1912 as the Garden of Allah. It had reopened in 1925 as the Circle Flying W. As soon as Chapman took ownership of the ranch, he constructed a new main building consisting of 10 rooms (shown here), which included a living room, dining room, kitchen, and six guest rooms. (Courtesy of Desert Caballeros Western Museum.)

The main building of the Lazy RC Ranch (shown here in another view) was considered modern, as it included hot and cold running water and electricity. In 1938, the ranch was sold to Frank Corwin from Phoenix. His wife, Zelma, and son Jim operated the ranch. (Courtesy of Desert Caballeros Western Museum.)

Wranglers are pictured here in the corrals at Lazy RC. In addition to a dude ranch, Frank Corwin ran a summer camp for boys where they learned to cook, ride horses, and round up cattle. In 1940, the Corwins closed the ranch to guests and leased it to several couples over the years. By 1986, it had become known as the Shady Pines: Palm Lake Guest Ranch and RV Park. The name was misleading, as it provided accommodations only for RVs and did not take guests. In 1987, the Nature Conservancy purchased the ranch, which is now the Hassayampa River Preserve. (Courtesy of Desert Caballeros Western Museum.)

The Triangle W ranch was originally homesteaded by the Bishop brothers in 1920. They homesteaded two side-by-side sections of 640 acres each. The house they built and shared was on the border of those two properties. The Bishops raised cattle and owned the Wickenburg butcher shop, where they sold meat from their ranch, then known as the C4. (Courtesy of Desert Caballeros Western Museum.)

This is an aerial view of the Triangle W Ranch. Between 1925 and 1937, the ranch changed hands several times. Despite the fact it had always been a cattle ranch, several attempts were made to take in guests. In 1936, Mrs. Edwin Bofferding purchased and completely renovated the ranch. A landing field that doubled as a polo field was also added. She called the ranch El Rancho del Sol. In 1939, Charles Williams purchased the ranch, renaming it Triangle W. (Courtesy of Desert Caballeros Western Museum.)

Charles Everett, manager and co-owner of the Triangle W Ranch, is pictured here holding guests' horses. The ranch closed at the beginning of World War II, as gasoline rationing prevented tourists from traveling. Steve and Evelyn Hambaugh purchased and reopened the Triangle W in 1944. In 1945, they sold to well-known Minnesota camp and hotel owner Brownie Cote, along with Fred Rogers and Charles Everett. Working with Squire Maguire, they donated 90 acres of the Triangle W to the Wickenburg Country Club for use as a golf course. This group also bought the Desert Willow Ranch in Tucson. The actress Irene Dunn was a guest, along with sports figures such as coach Bud Wilkinson. (Courtesy of Desert Caballeros Western Museum.)

This is a 1965 photograph of Jim and Denise Condren at the Lazy Fox Ranch. Col. Clinton Fox and his wife, Dorothy, bought the Triangle W in 1956, changing the name to the Lazy Fox. Much of the original land had been sold off for development. The Foxes operated the ranch until they sold to Remuda Ranch, an eating disorder facility that uses it for outpatients. (Courtesy of Desert Caballeros Western Museum.)

The main building of the Monte Vista Ranch (interior shown here) was erected on land originally settled in 1889 by Belisario Castro, who built a stage stop, bar, and store. In 1922, Lewis "Bob" White came to Arizona to recover from tuberculosis. Once he had recovered, White went to work for Romaine Lowdermilk at the Kay El Bar Ranch. White briefly partnered with Jack Burden (whom he had met when they were both guests at Circle Flying W) in the Remuda Ranch until Burden married Sophie Fletcher. In 1926, White purchased 120 acres and built the Monte Vista. (Courtesy of Desert Caballeros Western Museum.)

This photograph shows a guest room at the Monte Vista Ranch. In addition to comfortable, modern accommodations, the ranch offered rodeos, badminton, tennis, croquet, trapshooting, hunting, and sightseeing trips. (Courtesy of Desert Caballeros Western Museum.)

Guests of the Monte Vista Ranch are shown here waiting to head out on a trail ride. For several summers, the Whites operated the M Bar V Ranch in Flagstaff, Arizona. The riding horses were driven from Wickenburg to Flagstaff, which took four to five days. In 1928, Bob White married Edith Taff, and she became the ranch hostess. (Courtesy of Desert Caballeros Western Museum.)

Guests in this photograph are enjoying a bonfire and social time. Monte Vista hosted many prominent guests, including Navy secretary Frank Knox, Supreme Court justice Robert H. Jackson, and US president Herbert Hoover. The Whites sold the ranch in 1946 to the first of three successive owners. One couple, Carl and Verna Beilen, were former guests. The ranch closed in 1965 and was eventually torn down. (Courtesy of Desert Caballeros Western Museum.)

The three White brothers—from left to right, Lewis "Bob," John, and Luke—posed for this photograph at Monte Vista Ranch. Bob was the dude rancher, John was the singer, and Luke returned to Washington, DC. (Courtesy of Desert Caballeros Western Museum.)

Henry Warbasse is shown with the Packard that was used to transport Kay El Bar Ranch guests from the railroad depot. Warbasse wanted to marry a local doctor's daughter, Christine. Her father said Warbasse needed to have a job first, so he decided to be a dude rancher. With help from a crew of Pima Indians, Warbasse made adobe bricks from ranch soil. During the 1920s, the lodge, dining room, and guest rooms were constructed from these adobes. (Courtesy of Desert Caballeros Western Museum.)

This photograph shows the first camp established at Kay El Bar Ranch. The lumber cabin was dug into the hill north of the present buildings. The cabin was later moved and was used as a toolhouse and horseshoeing shed. It was last used as a gift shop. Romaine Lowdermilk, from Kansas, wanted to homestead 160 acres on the Hassayampa River. He was too young to file a claim, so he sat on his chosen property until his birthday. Lowdermilk later expanded the ranch to 640 acres. (Courtesy of Desert Caballeros Western Museum.)

Seen here are the original 1914 adobe buildings. A five-bedroom adobe house was added in 1918 to accommodate guests. In 1925, Romaine Lowdermilk formed a partnership with Henry Warbasse to develop the Kay El Bar Ranch into a dude ranch. Lowdermilk sold his interest to Warbasse in 1927. (Courtesy of Desert Caballeros Western Museum.)

Romaine Lowdermilk is shown doing rope tricks, as he often did at Kay El Bar Ranch and nearby Remuda Ranch. He would regularly do these tricks standing on a wire. During 1918, Lowdermilk became friends with the White brothers—Bob, John, and Luke. John was a Western singer who became the Lonesome Cowboy on NBC's *Death Valley Days*. John also wrote the book *Git Along, Little Dogies: Songs and Songmakers of the American West*. About the same time, Lowdermilk was singing Western music on a Phoenix radio station and writing songs. (Courtesy of Desert Caballeros Western Museum.)

Below, guests are shown riding out of the center of the Kay El Bar Ranch. A series of owners came and went during the 1940s, 1950s, and 1960s. In the late 1960s, Robert Kratville and Eugene Kilmer bought the ranch. Eugene's son, actor Val Kilmer, shared a room with his brother in what is now called Casa Monterrey. (Courtesy of Desert Caballeros Western Museum.)

A Kay El Bar Ranch ride through the Hassayampa River is pictured here. The ranch was designated a National Historic Place in the 1970s. Two sisters, Jane Nash and Jan Martin, who grew up as "dudes" at Upstate New York ranches, bought the ranch and ran it successfully for 17 years. In 1997, John and Nancy Loftis, former guests of dude ranches in Colorado, bought the historic ranch, which they renovated and redecorated. It is currently closed. (Courtesy of Desert Caballeros Western Museum.)

The Slash Bar K pool and arena are seen in this 1950s photograph. The arena served as the venue for rodeos, including the 1953 Desert Sun Ranch Association Rodeo in which five dude ranches participated. Rodeo stock for roping and bronc riding were kept on the ranch. (Courtesy of Desert Caballeros Western Museum.)

Pictured here in 1950, Don and Margie Kerr of Chicago owned the Slash Bar K from 1946 to 1955. Bob White originally sold the property to guests at his Monte Vista Ranch, Vernon and Lena Knight. The Kerrs started the dude ranch, eventually expanding from 3 to 24 rooms. (Courtesy of Desert Caballeros Western Museum.)

This is an aerial view of the main lodge of the Slash Bar K Ranch. In 1955, the ranch was sold to George and Grace Brown from Palm Springs, California. George had a successful career in the movie business with connections that brought several famous actors to the ranch, including Alan Ladd, William Bendix, and Bill Demarest. From 1958 to 1971, there were several owners and lessees of the ranch. In 1971, the ranch was sold to the Meadows, a rehabilitation center. (Courtesy of Desert Caballeros Western Museum.)

This photograph of the Bar FX Ranch includes riders, the ranch carriage, and the Hopi Lodge, which contained a large living room with a log-beamed ceiling and a huge stone fireplace. The ranch was started by F.X. "Foxy" O'Brien in the early 1900s as an experimental farm that included cement-lined irrigation ditches. The ranch was also leased by Leo and Nell Weaver, who briefly operated the Circle Flying W there as a dude ranch. Jack Burden and Bob White operated the Remuda Ranch on this property as well. Both groups moved their operations to other properties. The ranch is currently part of the Simpson Ranch, a cattle operation. (Courtesy of Desert Caballeros Western Museum.)

This is Henry Wickenburg's home, which became part of the Bar FX Ranch. It was known for the escape tunnel under the floor to be used in the case of an attack from the Apaches. (Courtesy of Desert Caballeros Western Museum.)

Wickenburg claimed to be the "Dude Ranch Capital of Arizona" until ranch numbers dwindled, and the town ceremoniously handed over the title to Tucson. Jack Burden of Remuda Ranch first contracted for this billboard outside of Wickenburg in 1941. (Courtesy of Desert Caballeros Western Museum.)

Sophie Burden's father, Dr. Fletcher, built this three-room bungalow on the Remuda Ranch for the Burden family. Soon, it was being rented out to guests, which meant Jack and Sophie's children—Sophie Jr., John, and Dana—often slept in the barn or under the stars. Jack Burden of Massachusetts had met Bob White of Washington, DC, as guests at the Circle Flying W. They both came to Arizona for their health. (Courtesy of Sophie Burden.)

In this Remuda Ranch photograph, Sophie Burden and her mother, Clementine Fletcher, show off the bull snake they are going to cook for the guests' dinner. Sophie met Jack Burden when her family became the very first guests at Remuda Ranch, located at the Bar FX at the time. The Fletchers stayed the whole first winter of operation. In 1926, Jack and Sophie married and bought out Bob White's interest. (Courtesy of Desert Caballeros Western Museum.)

From left to right, Dave Wheeler, Bill Keeler, and Sophie and John Burden pose for this photograph. In 1928, Jack and Sophie Burden moved the Remuda operation to 720 acres they had bought along both sides of the Hassayampa River. From 1928 to 1969, the Burden family expanded and improved their ranch. The first tennis court in Arizona was built there. The ranch had its own accredited school, a heated swimming pool, and a 4,000-foot airstrip. Famous guests who stayed at Remuda included Robert Mitchum, Erle Stanley Gardner, and Joel McCrea. In 1985, the ranch became the Remuda Ranch Eating Disorders Treatment Center. (Courtesy of Sophie Burden.)

Dana Burden is shown driving the Remuda Ranch touring car in this 1940s photograph. Dana was the youngest of Jack and Sophie's children. It all began in 1925 when Jack Burden and Bob White dropped off brochures for their new dude ranch at the local chamber of commerce. At the same time, the Fletcher family was there, looking for a place to stay. Jack and Bob invited them to their new dude ranch that was still just a concept, with no furniture, supplies, or food. They quickly bought all they needed and were ready when the Fletchers showed up the next day. (Courtesy of Sophie Burden.)

This photograph shows Remuda Ranch's Out Wickenburg Way Rodeo. Jack Burden started this rodeo in 1930. From this annual rodeo, world champion Everett Bowman and other cowboys had the base from which to establish the Cowboys' Turtle Association, the forerunner of the Professional Rodeo Cowboys Association (PRCA), which remains the most important group in rodeo. (Author's collection.)

This 1948 photograph shows the custom copper fireplace hood in the newly built Rancho de los Caballeros lodge. In 1943, Sylvia and Charles "Squire" Maguire and Rowena and Belford "Boff" Howard met as guests at Remuda Ranch. They soon dreamed of building their own ranch, but only if Dallas and Edie Gant would join them as working partners. At the time, Dallas was managing the Remuda Ranch for the Burdens. (Courtesy of Desert Caballeros Western Museum.)

A square dance is seen here in the Rancho de los Caballeros living room, now fully furnished. The custom-made furniture was based on the designs of Santa Fe craftsman Bruce Cooper. Once the ranch could afford it, Cooper came in to restyle the interiors, building much of the furniture in the bar patio. In addition to the main building, which included the living room, dining room, saloon, and office, the original construction consisted of 40 guest rooms, an oval swimming pool, a tennis court, barns, corrals, employee housing, and the Gant family house. During the early days, Bill Boyd (Hopalong Cassidy), Cary Grant, and Anne Baxter were guests of the ranch. (Courtesy of Desert Caballeros Western Museum.)

Santa comes to Rancho de los Caballeros. Christmas always had a significant place in the traditions of "De Los Cab," as the ranch is often called. Dallas Gant died suddenly of a cerebral hemorrhage in 1967 at only 54 years old. Edie took over management of the ranch. By 1970, all the Gants' partners had died or sold to Rusty and Susan Gant (Dallas and Edie's children). (Courtesy of Desert Caballeros Western Museum.)

This "dudeo" was held at Rancho de los Caballeros. The first inter-ranch rodeo where guests from the Wickenburg area ranches competed against each other occurred in 1951. Dudeos were a popular and long-running tradition in Wickenburg. (Courtesy of Desert Caballeros Western Museum.)

Pictured here is the original bar at Rancho de los Caballeros. In 1960, the ranch obtained a liquor license, and the bar was expanded. The ranch was originally conceived to be a comfortable, even luxurious destination at an authentic ranch setting. Steady improvement and expansion, including golf in 1980, as well as holding on to its traditions, made Rancho de los Caballeros very successful. The Gant family celebrated 50 years of owning and operating the ranch in 1998. (Courtesy of Desert Caballeros Western Museum.)

This photograph shows a fly-in at the Flying E Ranch's 3,500-foot dirt landing strip in March 1958. The Welliks discovered the ranch from the air in a plane. George was a pilot, and Vi was his navigator. As they flew over the property, Vi noted that it looked just like a "motel in the desert." They were headed to Texas but decided to land and check out the property. Eventually, they bought the ranch and spent the rest of their lives there. (Courtesy of Flying E Ranch.)

This 1960 Flying E Ranch photograph is labeled as "Our Gang." From left to right are Jack Switzer on Slippers, Wendy Wellik on Snowflake, Everett Bowman on Trixie, George Wellik, Vi Wellik, Cora, Warren Wellik, Eric (dog), Mary, Abby, Kay, and Claude. (Courtesy of Flying E Ranch.)

Flying E wrangler "brands" fellow wrangler and 1960–1961 world champion cowboy Everett Bowman, who was the first living cowboy to be named to the Cowboy Hall of Fame. Vi Wellik, owner from 1951 until her death in 2004, estimated that there were hundreds of guests with "branded britches" all over the country. (Courtesy of Flying E Ranch.)

The Flying E Ranch stagecoach transports guests from the train depot to the ranch in this 1953 photograph. The coach originally came out of the California goldfields and was used by the American Stage Company during the 1870s. The ranch also used the stage as a school bus and a shuttle for shopping in Wickenburg. In 1979, Vi Wellik donated the stage to the Desert Caballeros Western Museum. (Courtesy of Flying E Ranch.)

The Flying E Ranch hosts a cookout around the bonfire, with the ranch chuckwagon in the background. Even at a barbecue, Flying E has a reputation for service, good food, and attention to every detail. (Courtesy of Flying E Ranch.)

The main lodge of the Wickenburg Inn and Tennis Ranch included antiques and authentic building components, such as ceiling beams that came from ranches throughout the West. Construction began in 1972, with the ranch opening in 1973. (Courtesy of Desert Caballeros Western Museum.)

This is an aerial view of the Wickenburg Inn and Tennis Ranch. The ranch was located at the center of what was Bob White's Rafter Lazy W Cattle Ranch. Bob and his wife, Edith, had put together 16,000 acres through homesteading and purchase. Most of that acreage was sold off before 1948. Three partners from Chicago—Jean Kempner, Warren Jackman, and Larry Martin—purchased the remaining 4,600 acres in 1968. (Courtesy of Desert Caballeros Western Museum.)

This photograph shows the interior of a guest room at the Wickenburg Inn and Tennis Ranch. The adobe bricks and hand-painted tiles were imported from Mexico. In 1978, the inn received two highly coveted awards: the four-star award from the Mobile Travel Guide and the AAA four-diamond resort rating. (Courtesy of Desert Caballeros Western Museum.)

These golf carts were given to Wickenburg Inn guests for transport to the rooms on the hill, as cars were banned on the property. Though tennis was featured, a varied horseback riding program existed as well. This ranch was the only one in the Wickenburg area to operate year-round. Ongoing money troubles meant that many of the original plans were never realized. Following its bankruptcy, television personality and entrepreneur Merv Griffin purchased the ranch and significantly improved it. Despite his efforts, the ranch never met expectations and was donated to a nonprofit organization and later closed. (Courtesy of Desert Caballeros Western Museum.)

Two

TUCSON AREA RANCHES

Tucson, considered one of the oldest continually inhabited cities in the United States, was laid out for the Spanish by Col. Hugo O'Conor in 1775. The Spanish, Mexican, Confederate, and United States flags have all flown over the town.

Real growth in the area came once the Apache Indian threat had mostly diminished. Ranching grew very quickly, along with the spread of prospecting and mining. On February 12, 1912, Arizona became the 48th state. Tucson's warm and dry climate was discovered to do wonders for tuberculosis patients, and several sanitariums were opened to care for them. People with other breathing difficulties came to Tucson just for the healthy climate. Tourists followed, and dude ranches developed throughout the area, with the 1940s and 1950s being the peak for ranch numbers. People began to move into the area, and development began to threaten the ranches. Many of the ranchers did not have much land of their own and depended on the vacant land surrounding them for riding. Once the land was developed, they were forced out. Others gave in to the increased value of their property and sold their ranches. The remaining Tucson ranches share the advantages of being among the farthest out, owning more land, and having Saguaro National Park as their neighbor.

One of the original buildings at Tanque Verde Ranch is pictured here in 1958. The oldest surviving business in the Tucson area, the ranch was founded in 1868 by Emilio Carrillo, who called his new ranch Cebadilla (Little Barley) after the barley he grew on his roof as insulation. Today, his homestead house overlooks the ranch's breakfast ride site. (Courtesy of Chandler Warden.)

This 1930s photograph shows beef hanging on the Tanque Verde Ranch porch. Emilio Carrillo was a successful cattle rancher, and rumor had it that he had gold hidden at his ranch. In 1904, bandits hanged Carrillo by a beam in the main house in a room now called the card room. Carrillo survived and kept his gold, but died in 1908 from complications of his ordeal. (Courtesy of Bob and Rita Cote.)

This guest cottage was photographed at Tanque Verde Ranch in 1934. Rafael Carrillo took over the ranch after Emilio's death. He sold to Jim Converse in the 1920s. At the time, the ranch was about 50,000 acres and extended from 2,000 feet to 8,000 feet in elevation. Converse changed the name to Tanque Verde (Green Tank). (Courtesy of Pomona Public Library.)

This 1930s photograph shows the corrals and main building at Tanque Verde Ranch. Although Jim Converse was a successful and innovative cattle rancher, he added guest accommodations in 1928 and opened as a dude ranch. Sometimes described as "wild" or "brash," Converse was a great storyteller and host. (Courtesy of Bob and Rita Cote.)

The corrals and tack room at Tanque Verde Ranch are seen in this 1958 photograph. Jim Converse was a very active dude rancher who was involved in the Southern Arizona Dude Ranch Association until he accidentally shot and killed Francisco Alcantar Romero. Converse was visiting friends at Victoria Ceyla's home, when according to Victoria's brother, Romero came into the house "a little loud." Converse stepped in front of him and fired his .22 pistol above his head in order to scare him. The gun, however, malfunctioned, and several shots were fired. Romero died, and Converse went to prison. (Courtesy of Bob and Rita Cote.)

The ramada at Tanque Verde Ranch is shown in this 1934 photograph. Exhausted from the shooting and prison, Converse sold the ranch to Brownie Cote in 1957. Brownie wanted a ranch with access to public land, ensuring the property's long-term future. (Courtesy of Pomona Public Library.)

Mary and Ernie Austin are pictured here with guest Jan Neubauer in 1960. Ernie was head wrangler at Tanque Verde Ranch from 1958 to 1964. (Courtesy of Chandler Warden.)

Chandler Warden is pictured in front of the Tanque Verde Ranch in 1958. The Cote family drew friends and guests of their Minnesota properties with them to their Arizona ranches. The Warden family started going to the Cote family camps in 1928, then followed the Cotes to Tanque Verde in 1958. Chandler later made Tucson his home, eventually becoming one of the most important philanthropists in the area. (Courtesy of Chandler Warden.)

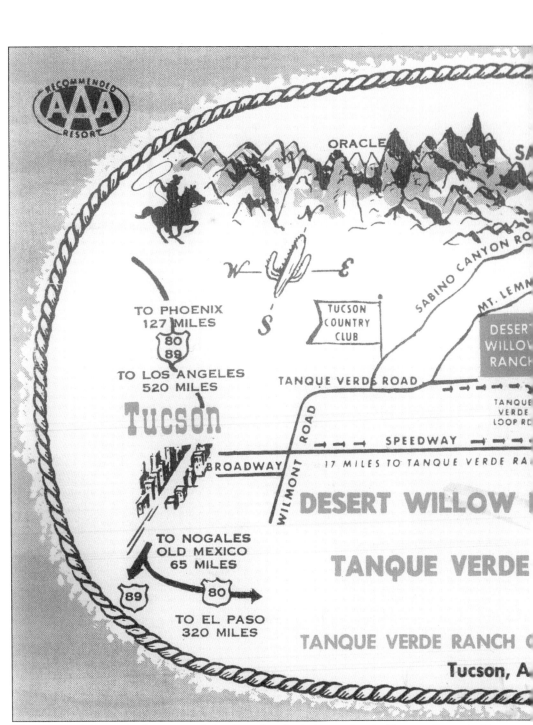

This postcard shows the locations of the Cote family dude ranches in Tucson. Brownie Cote entered hospitality in the 1920s when he bought two summer camps in northern Minnesota. In 1937, he added the Minnesota resort Grand View Lodge. In 1945, the Cotes purchased Triangle

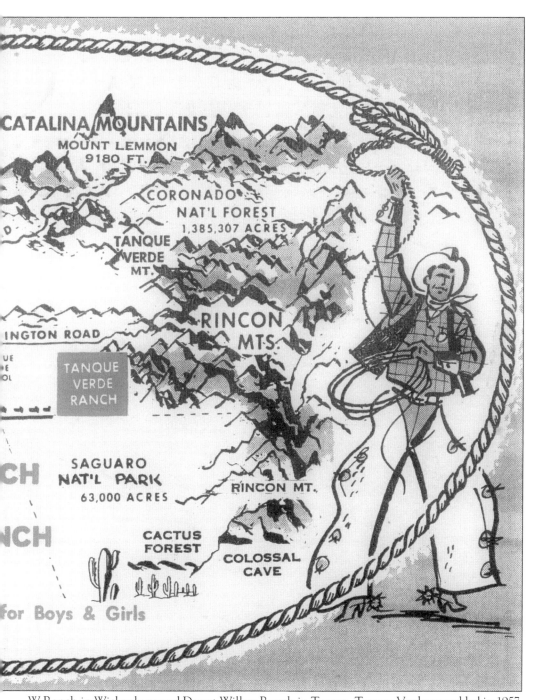

W Ranch in Wickenburg and Desert Willow Ranch in Tucson. Tanque Verde was added in 1957. (Courtesy of Chandler Warden.)

Brownie and Judy Cote, who came to Arizona in 1945 to provide year-round employment for their workforce, ultimately became the biggest name in Arizona dude ranching. (Courtesy of Bob and Rita Cote.)

Bob and Rita Cote check in guests at their Tanque Verde Ranch. Bob was coaxed back to the ranch in 1969 and improved and expanded it to one of the biggest and most well-known ranches in the United States. Bob pioneered international dude ranch marketing and the idea that Tucson was a year-round destination. In 2005, he was the first and only dude rancher inducted into Arizona's Hall of Fame for Tourism. In 2012, he was inducted into the Dude Ranchers' Hall of Fame. (Courtesy of Bob and Rita Cote.)

This 1903 photograph shows the original adobe homestead house that George Wilson bought in 1911. Eventually, the Wilsons named the ranch Rancho Linda Vista (Beautiful View Ranch). George Wilson had come to the Oracle area of Arizona in 1906 to recover from a baseball injury near his lung. Like so many, he found the area good for his health, and he decided to make it his home. (Courtesy of Chuck Sternberg/Rancho Linda Vista.)

A ride heads out from Rancho Linda Vista. Henry Bockman, a miner from the Oracle area, homesteaded the original property around 1882. He built a small home, dug a well, and constructed corrals, all to support his cattle operation. Bockman later sold the ranch to Charles Henry Bayless of Kansas. A university professor in Kansas, Bayless became very prominent and successful in Arizona as a cattle and sheep rancher, University of Arizona regent, banker, Pima County supervisor, business owner, and patron of the arts. (Courtesy of Chuck Sternberg/Rancho Linda Vista.)

This 1930s postcard image shows Rancho Linda Vista cowboy Fred Acevado and an unidentified guest in an iconic pose. (Courtesy of Chuck Sternberg/Rancho Linda Vista.)

This photograph from the late 1930s shows three female guests (sometimes called "dudines" in the early days of dude ranching) at the Rancho Linda Vista corral. George Wilson ran Rancho Linda Vista as a cattle ranch from 1911 until the family sold the dude ranch part of the property in 1958. The original ranch was 160 acres. The Wilsons eventually controlled between 125,000 and 150,000 acres, where they ran 1,500 cattle. (Courtesy of Chuck Sternberg/Rancho Linda Vista.)

Boyd Wilson, the manager of Rancho Linda Vista, is seen third from left, with a rope on his saddle. Boyd was George and Carlotta Wilson's second son. George had met Carlotta "Lottie" Gonzales at a wedding dance held at the Mountain View Hotel in Oracle. In 1912, Carlotta joined George on the ranch, where they initially lived in primitive conditions. Their first son, Thomas, was born in 1913. (Courtesy of Chuck Sternberg/ Rancho Linda Vista.)

Dudes and horses are seen at the barn of Rancho Linda Vista in the 1920s. The dude ranch operation opened in 1925. The early 1920s brought a drought and cattle losses to the area, which financially challenged the ranch. A guest and noted author, Harold Bell Wright, was staying on part of the ranch and suggested the Wilsons take in guests. Though skeptical, the Wilsons borrowed money to expand and improve the main building and to construct cabins. (Courtesy of Chuck Sternberg/Rancho Linda Vista.)

This photograph from the mid-1930s gives an overall view of Rancho Linda Vista. Harold Bell Wright had come to the ranch to research and write *The Mine with the Iron Door*, based on a legendary mine in the Catalina Mountains. The book was a success, and Wright demanded the movie be filmed on the ranch. (Courtesy of Chuck Sternberg/Rancho Linda Vista.)

Mules pack in the winter wood for Rancho Linda Vista in this 1929 photograph. The dude ranch that eventually grew to take 65 guests remained a working cattle ranch throughout the Wilson years. To this day, the San Carlos Apaches come down every year to harvest the acorns, and the Tohono O'Odham still harvest grass for their famous baskets. (Courtesy of Chuck Sternberg/ Rancho Linda Vista.)

The main lodge of the Rancho Linda Vista is shown in this mid-1950s photograph. During this time, the ranch was a well-known and very successful dude and cattle ranch. The success of the guest operation had all started when *The Mine with the Iron Door* movie was filmed at the ranch. Widespread fame and famous people followed, with a list that included Vice Pres. Charles Dawes, Tom Dewey, Clark Gable, Rita Hayworth, and Gary Cooper. (Courtesy of Chuck Sternberg/ Rancho Linda Vista.)

Fall branding at Rancho Linda Vista is pictured here. As one of the Tucson area's early dude ranches, Rancho Linda Vista was initially a working cattle ranch. The guests were offered the opportunity to help the cowboys in their work. Some guests jumped in, while others chose to watch. In all cases, the very real work of a cattle ranch was a big part of the guests' experience. (Courtesy of Chuck Sternberg/ Rancho Linda Vista.)

This photograph shows Rancho Linda Vista in 1968, just after the Rancho Linda Vista Community of the Arts (formed as ETA Trust) purchased the ranch. George Wilson died in 1957, and his son Tom sold the cattle operation to Lloyd Golder in 1960. The dude ranch and 80 acres were sold to the Tres Amigos Guest Ranch Company. ETA Trust bought the ranch out of foreclosure in 1968. The concept of the ranch as an art community is attributed to artist and University of Arizona professor Charles Littler, who considered the ranch his "major work of art." (Courtesy of Chuck Sternberg/Rancho Linda Vista.)

This 1974 photograph shows the people of Rancho Linda Vista Community of the Arts. Though membership has changed significantly since 1968, the community members believe they have had "a remarkable continuity of shape and style over the years." Along with their families, the residents of the ranch are artists or those with a strong interest in the arts. The community includes artists from many different media, and as such, it sponsors many different art events. (Courtesy of Chuck Sternberg/Rancho Linda Vista.)

This is an early photograph of the Flying V Ranch with an especially beautiful cristate saguaro in the center. The ranch started out as a mining claim in the Catalina Mountain foothills. It was then homesteaded sometime before Arizona became a state in 1912. In 1915, the ranch hosted Harold Bell Wright, who would later write *The Mine with the Iron Door* while staying at Rancho Linda Vista in Oracle. He had come to Tucson to recover from tuberculosis. (Courtesy of Arizona Historical Society, BN201580.)

Two cowboys on horseback enter the Ventana Creek near the Flying V Ranch in 1920. The working cattle ranch comprised about 25,000 acres of deeded and leased land. A dude ranch operation was added in 1928. R.C. and Betty Lowry owned the ranch during the 1920s. The ranch continued to run cattle until the 1960s. (Courtesy of Arizona Historical Society, BN201387.)

Polo players are shown at the Flying V Ranch, which boasted a "full size, sideboarded polo field," according to the 1938–1939 *Tucson Recreation* publication. The ranch maintained a string of polo ponies, and several practice games were available weekly to guests. (Courtesy of Arizona Historical Society, BN201582.)

These 1930 photographs show the interior and exterior of guest accommodations at the Flying V Ranch. The dude ranch started modestly with rock and adobe cabins. The first improvement was the addition of hot and cold running water to the guest rooms. Tennis courts were added later. In a 1943 newspaper article, the ranch claimed the largest and best private rodeo arena in the Southwest. In addition, the Flying V maintained its own bucking horses, riding steers, roping calves, and other rodeo stock. The guests were able to watch cowboys practice rodeo several times a week. A competition rodeo was held every Sunday of the season, and guests were also able to compete in weekly "arena games." (Both, courtesy of Arizona Historical Society; above, BN201597; below, BN201603.)

A group of riders heads out from the lodge at Flying V Ranch in 1936. One of the ranch activities described in the ranch's 1930s brochure was the "bandit hunt." A ranch cowboy was the bandit, with the guests riding out as the posse to capture him. Occasionally, the bandit would appear on a hilltop, eventually leading the guests on "a wild, roaring, steeplechase all over the ranch until he was caught." (Courtesy of Pomona Public Library.)

At Flying V Ranch, guests are shown all "duded up" and posing for the camera. Lynn Gillham owned the Flying V from 1930 until 1947, when John and Josephine Shields bought the ranch. The ranch was known for its overnight pack trips high into the Catalina Mountains and twice weekly all-day rides. The Shieldses maintained the existing operation for as long as they could, but in 1979, the surrounding development made dude ranching impossible and the ranch offered cabin rentals only. (Courtesy of Arizona Historical Society, BN201588.)

Here is the entrance gate to the Double R Ranch. The ranch was built on land along the Sabino Creek that was once farmed by Native Americans. Later, the area was part of a large cattle operation. Over time, parcels were sold off, and in 1935, the remaining land became a dude ranch, originally named Double R Ranch. (Courtesy of Pomona Public Library.)

Guests are enjoying the Tucson weather in this 1936 photograph of the Double R Ranch, later called the Double U Ranch. (Courtesy of Pomona Public Library.)

The front drive and lodge of the Double R Ranch are pictured here. In the first three years as a dude operation, the ranch was called the Double R. The name was changed to Double U in 1938. (Courtesy of Arizona Historical Society, BN201672.)

A living room at the Double U Ranch is seen in this 1939 photograph. During the 1940s, ranch owner Armand Retter was active in the Southern Arizona Dude Ranch Association. During the 1960s, the same was true for owner Bertha Mahler. (Courtesy of Pomona Public Library.)

This 1939 photograph shows a guest cottage in the early days of the Double U Ranch, which was an active and often-mentioned member of the Tucson dude ranch community. (Courtesy of Pomona Public Library.)

A guest accommodation at the Double U Ranch is shown here in 1939. The ranch steadily expanded and improved during the 1940s and 1950s until, in 1960, it could accommodate 60 guests, making it one of the largest dude ranches in the Tucson area. The ranch was also a filming location for *Arizona* and *Billy the Kid*. (Courtesy of Pomona Public Library.)

This image from a 1960s Double U brochure shows the quality of food offered by the more upscale dude ranches. Almost all ranches were "Full American Plan," which meant that food was included in the rate. (Author's collection.)

DOUBLE U RANCH, TUCSON, ARIZONA

Two guests soak up the Arizona sun at the Double U Ranch. In 1939, the ranch followed the traditional Southern Arizona season, from November to April. With no air-conditioning, it was not possible to host guests during the summer months. In 1966, Phil Rothschild purchased the ranch, and his family remained the owners until it was sold to the Zuckermans in 1978. (Courtesy of Pomona Public Library.)

Guests play Ping-Pong and croquet in this 1939 photograph of the Double U Ranch. The beauty of the ranch convinced Mel and Enid Zuckerman that they had found the location to build their own groundbreaking vision of a health spa. From these 39 rooms, public buildings, horse facilities, swimming pool, and tennis courts sprang Canyon Ranch, what is now the most acknowledged and renowned health spa brand in the world. (Courtesy of Pomona Public Library.)

The mounting corral of the Desert Willow Ranch is pictured here with a backdrop of the Catalina Mountains. The ranch allowed guests to ride alone (without a wrangler) "once they became familiar with the surrounding country and at home with their mounts." (Courtesy of Bob and Rita Cote.)

DESERT WILLOW RANCH   TUCSON, ARIZONA

Big, beautiful saguaro cacti frame this photograph of guests out on a ride at Desert Willow Ranch. The area where they are riding, and nearly all the open land seen in this image, has been developed as the growth of Tucson pushed out many of the ranches. (Courtesy of Bob and Rita Cote.)

Pictured here is the putting green at Desert Willow Ranch. The ranch was opened in 1934, and it was expanded and upgraded over time. By the 1940s, the ranch had added tennis, lawn games, a swimming pool, target ranges, and an extensive recreation room to its offerings. (Courtesy of Bob and Rita Cote.)

These are guest accommodations at Desert Willow Ranch. During the 1940s and 1950s, the Dude Ranch Rodeo Association held its rodeos at Desert Willow and also at El Carnilla Ranch. These were real rodeos in which ranch owners, employees, and guests all competed. In 1947, the group picked a rodeo queen from among the guests. (Courtesy of Bob and Rita Cote.)

The pool at Desert Willow Ranch is seen here from above. In 1945, Brownie Cote and Chuck Everett purchased the ranch from Jack Mulcahy, who had owned it for four years. At about the same time, the partners purchased the Triangle W in Wickenburg. The Desert Willow became one of the most successful ranches in Tucson until it closed in 1968. (Courtesy of Bob and Rita Cote.)

Safford (Sombrero) Peak is centered between the saguaro cacti in this photograph of Saguaro Vista Ranch. Ranch legend claims a local bandit called "Tejano" hid out on or around Safford Peak and descended to rob stages on the nearby Butterfield Stage route. The story goes on to say that the original stone fireplace contains the map to where Tejano hid the $50,000 in gold he had stolen from the Army payroll stage. (Courtesy of Mira Vista Resort.)

The pool at Saguaro Vista Ranch is seen in the center of this photograph. At right in the background is the main lodge, which, though much expanded, includes the original building. Because the ranch had a well, it was often a stop for travelers in the area during the 1860s and 1870s. The well is now the Mira Vista Resort's Jacuzzi. (Author's collection.)

Charles and Lily Elkins are pictured in front of their Saguaro Vista Ranch in 1953. They originally called the ranch Giant Beauty. On February 20, 1936, they opened the ranch as Saguaro Vista. (Courtesy of Mira Vista Resort.)

Pictured here is one of the stone and adobe guest accommodations at the Saguaro Vista Ranch. The ranch became a destination for Hollywood legends, including John Wayne, Greta Garbo, Cary Grant, and Katharine Hepburn. In the 1980s, the ranch was used as a treatment center for addictive behavior. The actress Suzanne Somers contributed her name and money to the institute. (Courtesy of Mira Vista Resort.)

The aerial view in this postcard shows the Saguaro Vista Ranch. In 1997, the Wolfe family purchased the ranch and made extensive renovations. They ran the property (then called La Tierra Linda) as a boutique resort and event center. In 2006, the ranch became Mira Vista Resort, a "clothing optional" property. Expansion and renovations followed, with the unique resort finding tremendous success. (Author's collection.)

The main ranch house at Rancho Robles is pictured here in 1936. Originally an impressive personal residence built and developed by Charles and Helen Gilliland from 1923 to 1927, this building served as the core for Rancho Robles, which opened as a dude ranch in 1935. (Courtesy of Pomona Public Library.)

The corrals and stables at Rancho Robles are pictured here in 1936. The ranch offered a variety of rides and pack trips into the Catalina Mountains. Extensive hunting options were offered, including bear, mountain lion, javelina, deer, coyote, duck, and other small game. Trips and activities in the nearby town of Oracle were also available. (Courtesy of Pomona Public Library.)

This 1936 photograph shows the living room in the main ranch house of Rancho Robles. The ranch operated between 1935 and 1956 with the names El Rancho Robles, El Rancho de los Robles, Rancho Vita, Hotel Rancho Vita, and Rancho Robles. From 1956 to 2012, the ranch was used as long-term rental homes. In 2012, Blake Campbell purchased the property, restored it, and reopened it as a guest ranch and retreat center. (Courtesy of Pomona Public Library.)

A festive gathering takes place at the Diamond W Ranch. The ranch got its start when George Westinghouse (of Westinghouse Electric) made several land purchases totaling 200 acres on Tanque Verde Road and constructed several buildings for family and friends. All this became one of the most active and recognized dude ranches in the Tucson area. Julia Bennett, the owner, also had a dude ranch in Montana called the Diamond J. (Courtesy of Arizona Historical Society, PC151f556425.)

The original house at Lazy K Bar Ranch is seen here in the 1940s. Elmer Staggs homesteaded the 160 acres in the Tucson Mountains in 1930s. The native stone building remains the core of the ranch's lodge. (Courtesy of Lazy K Bar Ranch.)

Above is an original adobe accommodation at Lazy K Bar Ranch. One of the biggest names in dude ranching, the Van Cleves of Montana bought the ranch in the late 1930s and built the first five guest rooms. The dude ranch opened in 1940. Three generations of Paul Van Cleves were presidents of the Dude Ranchers' Association. (Courtesy of Lazy K Bar Ranch.)

This 1940s photograph shows the interior of the original homestead building at Lazy K Bar Ranch. The man is unidentified. The Van Cleveses, who had started the ranch using the name from their famous Montana ranch, found the twice-annual moves to be too much. They sold the ranch to Florence Louise Clarey in April 1944. The name was changed to the Clarey Ranch. (Courtesy of Lazy K Bar Ranch.)

The guest cottages at Lazy K Bar Ranch are shown in this 1940s photograph. In 1946, Florence Louise Clarey sold the ranch to Carl and Evie Krah, who immediately changed the name back to Lazy K Bar Ranch. Carl, a graduate of Yale University and veteran of World War I, died in 1950. (Courtesy of Lazy K Bar Ranch.)

A guest accommodation at Lazy K Bar Ranch is pictured in this 1940s photograph. Views across the Tucson valley show both the Tortolita and Santa Catalina mountain ranges. Tucked in against the Tucson Mountains, the ranch had nearly unlimited riding all the way to the Santa Cruz River and back into what is now Saguaro National Park. (Courtesy of Lazy K Bar Ranch.)

Irv and Doris Spaulding (right) are pictured with two unidentified guests at Lazy K Bar Ranch in 1960. They had purchased the ranch in 1958. Irv died fairly soon after this photograph was taken, and Doris and her daughter Gail ran the ranch. The Spauldings also raced horses at the local Rillito Racetrack. The ranch was leased to two different operators, then sold to Bob and Jean Machold in 1968. (Courtesy of Carol Moore.)

Lazy K Bar Ranch is seen in this aerial view from the late 1940s. The Macholds, from Connecticut, bought the ranch after visiting it as guests. They sold to Milroy and Rosemary Blowitz in 1975. The Blowitzes ran the ranch together with longtime manager Carol Moore until it was sold in 1999 and closed in 2006. (Courtesy of Lazy K Bar Ranch.)

This 1941 photograph shows a guest cottage at Wild Horse Ranch, founded and opened in 1940 by Howard and Grace Miller. Their brochure details its history as a cattle ranch homesteaded in the 1920s. Wild Horse might have originally been the Eureka Ranch that took guests from 1938 to 1939. (Courtesy Pomona Public Library.)

Idaho senator Glen Taylor is shown at Wild Horse Ranch in this 1947 press photograph. The ranch had a long list of distinguished guests, including John Wayne, Jimmy Stewart, Art Linkletter, Virginia Mayo, Gary Cooper, Paul Newman, and an archduke of Austria. (Author's collection.)

The bar at Wild Horse Ranch is pictured in this brochure image. Socializing was central to the dude ranch experience from the beginning. Many ranches controlled who could be a guest by requiring references. In the 1960s, the Millers added "Club" to the ranch name to maintain the legal right to restrict who could stay there. (Author's collection.)

This brochure image shows the dining room at Wild Horse Ranch. The Miller family knew the importance of good food and maintained high standards. Like many ranches of that era, they required their guests to dress for dinner. (Author's collection.)

A Wild Horse Ranch trail ride is shown in this photograph. Because of its location near the Tucson Mountains, Wild Horse Ranch and other neighboring ranches conducted rides extensively in what is now Saguaro National Park. (Author's collection.)

Below are Howard and Grace Miller, founders and owners of Wild Horse Ranch. Howard was a very active leader in dude ranching. Only two years after opening his ranch, he helped found the Southern Arizona Dude Ranch Association and served as its first president in 1942. He was president again in 1947. Howard was a tireless advocate for dude ranching's importance and economic impact. He also stressed the importance of cooperation and advertising. (Author's collection.)

This Wild Horse Ranch publicity photograph has a dude enjoying the music of a singing cowboy. Nearly all ranches included musical entertainment in the lodges or around the bonfires. (Courtesy of Arizona Historical Society, HS56428.)

The pool at Wild Horse Ranch is pictured below. After achieving success with their ranch, the Millers stepped back from the helm in the 1950s, and their daughter-in-law Lona became the driving force behind the ranch until it was sold in 1979. The ranch, now called the Oasis at Wild Horse Ranch, serves as a popular wedding and event venue. (Author's collection.)

Westward Look's original building is seen behind the trees in this photograph of the ranch pool. William and Maria Watson built this hacienda-style home six months after Arizona became a state in 1912. Today, the living room of the Watsons' home is Westward Look's Vigas Room, named for the exposed log beams. (Courtesy of Westward Look.)

This is another view of the main lodge at Westward Look, with a rearing horse and rider entertaining guests in the foreground. The 1920s brought more tourists to Tucson, and the Watsons added 15 cottages around their original home. It is not known what the name of the ranch was at this time. (Courtesy of Westward Look.)

This photograph shows Dean Martin's favorite room at Westward Look. The singer and actor hosted the Tucson Open Golf Tournament from 1972 to 1975. (Courtesy of Westward Look.)

A horseback rider greets a car at the entrance to the expanded lodge of Westward Look. Bob and Beverly Nason, owners of the ranch in the 1940s, named their thriving dude ranch Westward Look after hearing an inspirational speech by Sir Winston Churchill on April 27, 1941, following the start of World War II. Churchill used the quote "but westward, look, the land is bright" (from Arthur Hugh Clough's "Say not the struggle naught availeth") in his speech to Britain. (Courtesy of Westward Look.)

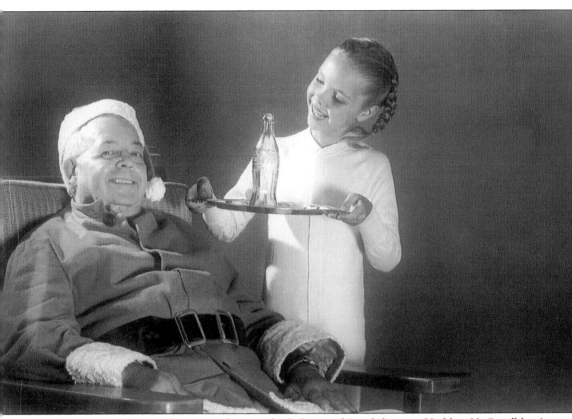

This image of Santa Claus was taken on the balcony of Swedish artist Haddon H. Sundblom's room at the Westward Look in the early 1930s. The Coca-Cola Company hired Sundblom to create a Santa that would be more appealing to children than the tall, thin, stern Kris Kringle of European creation. Between 1931 and 1966, the artist produced 40 paintings for Coca-Cola that would define the image of Santa Claus. A 1953 article in *Refresher* magazine shows the artist and his models Lani and Sancy Nason, daughters of the Westward Look owners, around his easel at Westward Look. Sundblom's old room is now a desert gallery with displays about Santa, the Nason girls, and the artist. (Courtesy of Westward Look.)

Westward Look is seen here from the air. The Nasons sold the ranch in the late 1960s. Over time, the dude ranch has become a world-renowned resort where its setting and respect for its history have set it apart. (Courtesy of Westward Look.)

This 1970s photograph shows the pool at Saddle and Surrey Ranch. Jim and Stell Webb built the property specifically to be a dude ranch in 1948, at which time it was called the Sun Circle Ranch. (Author's collection.)

The pool at Saddle and Surrey Ranch is seen from another view in this image from a 1970s brochure. In 1953, Virgil and Doris Jackson purchased the ranch and renamed it Saddle and Surrey. Virgil and Doris ran the ranch, along with their son Jack and his wife, Colette. Jack was very active and involved in local and state boards and associations. Colette appears on the cover of the February 13, 1956, *Newsweek* magazine. The Jacksons sold to Cottonwood de Tucson, a substance abuse treatment center, in 1987. (Author's collection.)

This 1930s photograph shows students arriving at the Hacienda del Sol School. Tucson developer John W. Murphey originally purchased the property at a public auction in 1928. The 7,000 acres were a combination of state and federal land perfectly located in the Catalina Mountain foothills. (Courtesy of Hacienda del Sol Guest Ranch Resort.)

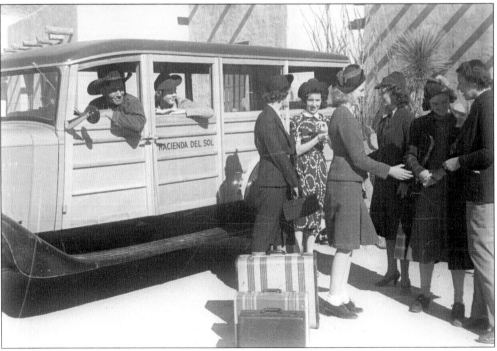

Hacienda del Sol students are pictured here in the 1930s. Original owners Helen and John Murphey had the ranch built in the Spanish Colonial architectural style. Helen even carved the intricate patterns on the library's ceiling. In the late 1930s, renowned Swiss architect Josiah Joesler designed the areas of the Hacienda that were rebuilt after a fire. (Courtesy of Hacienda del Sol Guest Ranch Resort.)

The girls' dorm rooms were located in this area of the main house at Hacienda del Sol School, seen here in the 1930s. The dorms later became guest rooms for the dude ranch that followed. (Courtesy of Hacienda del Sol Guest Ranch Resort.)

A student of the Hacienda del Sol is pictured with her horse in the Western wear of the school. The Hacienda was a college preparatory school that admitted about 28 girls at any one time. Each girl had her own horse. Girls from the Pillsbury, Vanderbilt, Maxwell, Westinghouse, Spalding, and Campbell families attended the nationally known school. (Courtesy of Hacienda del Sol Guest Ranch Resort.)

This aerial view of Hacienda del Sol Ranch shows the open space in 1949. This area has since been developed with homes and a major resort. In 1948, Hacienda del Sol opened as a guest ranch. The owners had Hollywood connections and hosted legendary celebrities as guests, including John Wayne, Katharine Hepburn, Spencer Tracy, Clark Gable, and Howard Hughes. Tracy's favorite room is still enjoyed by guests today. (Courtesy of Hacienda del Sol Guest Ranch Resort.)

The Catalina Mountains serve as a backdrop for this view of the pool at Hacienda del Sol Ranch. The pool was added in 1949. Robert Hartman and his wife, Bernice, purchased the ranch in the 1970s and maintained very high standards at their property, which they referred to as a "resort ranch." They were awarded both four diamonds from AAA and four stars from Mobil. Hartman had risen from dishwasher to management in the Cote family business before owning the Hacienda. (Courtesy of Hacienda del Sol Guest Ranch Resort.)

Above is the Hacienda del Sol living room from the 1930s, and below is the dining room as it appeared in 1970. The Hartmans sold the ranch in the 1980s when extensive surrounding development made dude ranching impossible. For several years, the ranch struggled and mostly failed as it changed hands and searched for its identity. In 1995, a group of local businesspeople bought the ranch and brought it back. This group quickly established the Grill restaurant, a favorite for fine dining in Tucson. The entire property was refreshed and renovated, while always maintaining the unique history and feel of the ranch. In 2014, the owners began a major expansion project, and today the property includes 59 rooms, a new ballroom, and an additional swimming pool and hot tub. (Both, courtesy of Hacienda del Sol Guest Ranch Resort.)

This photograph from the 1930s or 1940s shows the main entrance to the Hacienda Del Sol ranch. The beautiful entry gate is still in place and might be among the most painted and photographed spots in Tucson. (Courtesy of Hacienda del Sol Guest Ranch Resort.)

Cowboys are shown branding a calf in the squeeze chute at the MZ Bar Ranch (now White Stallion Ranch) in the 1950s. The ranch was homesteaded by David Young in 1936. He found an adobe home, well, and corrals on what was then federal land. It was essentially a "squatter's ranch" at the time he homesteaded. The next owner, Herbert Bruning, called his cattle ranch the CB Bar. (Courtesy of White Stallion Ranch.)

Max "the Hat" Zimmerman of Zimmerman's Liquors in downtown Chicago (billed as the "largest in the world") established the MZ Bar Ranch in 1945. He bought the cattle, chicken, and turkey ranch and went on to build the line of cottages and expand the old ranch house before opening the dude ranch to guests. This aerial view from 1946 shows the chicken and turkey sheds (center right), as well as the oval cattle cistern that served as the ranch swimming pool. (Courtesy of White Stallion Ranch.)

A donkey is shown pulling a two-wheel cart in front of the pump house, windmill, and tack room at the MZ Bar Ranch in this 1950s photograph. Max Zimmerman had sold the ranch to Mary Varner and her sister Victoria in 1949. (Courtesy of White Stallion Ranch.)

Mary Varner (center right), owner of MZ Bar Ranch, is pictured with guests of her ranch in the 1950s. Varner operated the MZ Bar as a guest ranch and as housing for officers based at the nearby Marana Army Air Field. In 1958, Brew and Marge Towne convinced Varner to sell the ranch to them. The Townes, from Massachusetts, had been guests at Lazy K Bar Ranch, located just over the mountains to the east. (Courtesy of White Stallion Ranch.)

Allen and Cynthia True are shown in front of the main lodge and dining room of their White Stallion Ranch in 1968. Cynthia lived in Denver, Colorado, her entire life until moving to the ranch. Born in Wyoming and raised in Montana, Allen was living in Denver when they went "all in" and bought the dude ranch outside Tucson, Arizona. (Courtesy of White Stallion Ranch.)

The 1968 press party for *High Chaparral*, a new television Western at the time, was held at White Stallion Ranch, which was used extensively as a location for the show from 1968 to 1972. The ranch has had at least 26 feature films, and countless television shows, commercials, and fashion shoots take advantage of the classic Arizona backdrops surrounding the property. Actors who have visited the ranch include George Clooney, Jimmy Stewart, James Garner, Glenn Close, Gene Autry, Tom Hanks, Robert Wagner, Robert Young, and Ronald Reagan. (Courtesy of White Stallion Ranch.)

This photograph from the early 1960s shows the main lodge at White Stallion Ranch. This building was comprised of the dining room, kitchen, bar, lodge, and five guest rooms. Completely renovated and redecorated, the entire building is now a dining space and public area. (Courtesy of White Stallion Ranch.)

The cookout site at White Stallion Ranch is pictured here in 1962. Located in the geographical center of the ranch, this spot offers full surrounding views. The mountain in the background is Safford Peak, named for the third territorial governor of Arizona. The mountain was part of the ranch until the mid-1980s, when it was traded to the National Park Service to become part of Saguaro National Park. The cookout area remains in use today. (Courtesy of White Stallion Ranch.)

Here, cattle are being loaded through the roping chute at White Stallion Ranch. Clyde Davis (center rear) was the ranch's head wrangler and mentor to the Trues' sons, Russell and Michael, teaching them to rope, break horses, and wrangle. (Courtesy of White Stallion Ranch.)

Russell True is pictured with Sancho, the trained longhorn steer, at the White Stallion Ranch in 1987. For more than 25 years, Sancho performed tricks and posed for photographs with ranch guests. Sancho was born on the ranch as part of the longhorn herd that has been at White Stallion since the 1960s. (Courtesy of White Stallion Ranch.)

Judy Bellini is shown babysitting Michael True in this 1968 photograph. Bellini was the first employee hired by Allen and Cynthia in 1965. Originally a waitress, she wrangled in addition to working in maintenance and transportation. After a few years of doing it all, Bellini finally settled in as a chef and celebrated her 50th year at the ranch, along with the Trues, in 2015. (Courtesy of Judy Bellini.)

Three

OTHER AREA RANCHES

Once dude ranching came to Arizona, the number of ranches spread throughout the state, with a concentration in Phoenix/Wickenburg and south. Frank Blaine Norris lists 52 ranches in the Phoenix area. Few survived the 1950s, and none were left by the end of the 1970s.

Some southern ranches have access to high-altitude mountain riding and, in fact, offer several thousand feet of elevation change where riders can start out among saguaro cacti and end up beneath ponderosa pines and aspen trees. Other ranches are located in the alpine areas of Northern and East-Central Arizona, where summer is their high season. With most dudes looking to the upper Rocky Mountain states for their summer vacation, these alpine ranches in Arizona have always had the challenge of getting the word out about their locations. Sprucedale, today's oldest continually operating ranch, has been the successful exception.

The rural dude ranches of Arizona are often smaller and sometimes simpler operations, built around the area and history that surround them. The traditions that have served this unique travel experience so well, so long, are clearer and less obscured at the rural ranches. The majority of Arizona's surviving ranches are these.

The cantina at Rancho de la Osa is shown in this 1930s photograph. Generally considered the oldest continually used building in Arizona, the cantina was constructed by Jesuit father Eusebio Franciscp Kino's missionary priests in the early 1700s. For its first century, it served as a trading post for local tribes and as a resting place for traveling missionaries. (Courtesy of Rancho de la Osa.)

Hundreds of cattle are shown in the corrals at Rancho de la Osa in this 1930s photograph. For most of the 1800s, the property was part of a large cattle ranch. Col. William Sturges of Chicago established the La Osa Ranch in 1889, and he spared no expense in building the hacienda, which featured imported wood floors and stained-glass windows. The gardens were 10 acres in size. (Courtesy of Rancho de la Osa.)

Horses roam in the corrals at Rancho de la Osa. The modern border with Mexico is seen in the background. In 1916, Pancho Villa rode north and attempted to capture the ranch during the Mexican Revolution. A cannonball from the attack was removed from the adobe and is now on display. (Courtesy of Rancho de la Osa.)

Riders pose in front of the hacienda at Rancho de la Osa. In 1924, historian Louisa Wetherill came south with her husband, John, looking for a lost tribe of Navajo Indians. She never found them but did create a dude ranch at the de la Osa. The Wetherills also had a dude ranch in Northern Arizona. Tom Mix and Zane Grey were frequent guests in those early days. (Courtesy of Rancho de la Osa.)

A courtyard scene at Rancho de la Osa is the subject of this photograph. In 1927, Arthur Hardgrave of Kansas City purchased the ranch as a birthday gift for his wife, Glenn. She was a guest at the ranch in 1926 and wrote a series of articles about her experiences there for the *Kansas City Journal Post.* (Courtesy of Arizona Historical Society, BN21415.)

This postcard view of Rancho de la Osa became an iconic image for this historic ranch. In 1935, a group of eastern investors bought the ranch, with Dick Jenkins as president and manager. Jenkins was elected as the second president of the Southern Arizona Dude Ranch Association. He was well known for hosting "cattle crossings" where invited guests watched while as many as 2,000 cattle were driven across the international border. (Courtesy of Arizona Historical Society, BN93192.)

A living room at Rancho de la Osa is shown in this 1930s photograph. The ranch closed for about three and a half years during World War II while Dick Jenkins served in the Army Air Corps. Dick's twin sister, Nellie, came out west to help run the ranch when it reopened in the fall of 1945. (Courtesy of Rancho de la Osa.)

Pres. Lyndon Johnson is seen on horseback at the Rancho de la Osa. Dick Jenkins became chairman of the Arizona Democratic Party, and many prominent Democrats were guests at his ranch, including Johnson, Adlai Stevenson, Franklin and Eleanor Roosevelt, and Hubert Humphrey. William Clayton drafted much of the Marshall Plan there in 1948. (Courtesy of Rancho de la Osa.)

Claudia Alta "Lady Bird" Johnson (right) poses in front of the original building at Rancho de la Osa. The other two people pictured are unidentified. Along with political figures, John Wayne, Cesar Romero, Joan Crawford, and Margaret Mitchell were guests at the ranch. (Courtesy of Rancho de la Osa.)

This 1930s photograph shows an outdoor fireplace at one of the Rancho de la Osa courtyards. Dick Jenkins died suddenly, and Nellie sold the ranch to a group of former guests in 1962. Evelyn Hamlen bought out the others and ran the ranch for 10 years. The Davis family owned and operated the ranch from 1981 to 1996. (Courtesy of Rancho de la Osa.)

The Rancho de la Osa cemetery is pictured below. Buried here are many of the people who have been a part of this ranch, a place that very well might be home to more history than anywhere else in Arizona. In 1996, Richard and Veronica Schultz bought the ranch and went to work restoring this irreplaceable property. The Schultzes retired and closed the ranch in 2014. (Courtesy of Rancho de la Osa.)

This photograph shows Faraway Ranch from above. Swedish immigrants Neil and Emma Erickson originally homesteaded the ranch in 1888. As their family grew to include three children—Lillian, Ben, and Hildegard—Neil transformed the one-room log cabin to a comfortable two-story house. (Courtesy of National Park Service.)

Lillian Erickson Riggs is shown in this Faraway Ranch photograph. Neil and Emma moved away in 1917, and Hildegard began offering rooms and meals to weekend boarders. Lillian gave up her teaching job and returned home to comanage the ranch. In 1918, the sisters expanded the ranch by purchasing the neighboring Stafford home. (Courtesy of National Park Service.)

A group of riders is pictured in front of the Faraway Ranch in the 1930s. Hildegard moved away in 1920, giving Lillian complete control of the ranch. Lillian married Ed Riggs in 1923. Together, they improved the ranch, adding indoor plumbing, a swimming pool, and more cottages. (Courtesy of National Park Service.)

Big Balanced Rock in Chiricahua National Monument is seen here in the 1940s. Lillian Riggs lost her eyesight in 1942 and was mostly deaf as well. Despite this, she continued to run Faraway Ranch and was considered a gracious host. Her husband, Ed, and her mother both died in 1950. With ranch manager J.P. "Andy" Anderson, Lillian continued on until 1970, when she closed the ranch. (Courtesy of National Park Service.)

This 1950s photograph shows the Faraway Ranch sign with an unidentified couple. Lillian and Ed Riggs campaigned for the establishment of the Chiricahua National Monument, which happened in 1924. Ed designed the hiking trail system with an eye to horseback riding. The ranch was sold to the federal government in 1979 and is included in the monument. Today, the National Park Service staff conducts tours of the ranch, which operated from 1917 to 1970. (Courtesy of National Park Service.)

This photograph shows Sprucedale Ranch as it appeared in 1930. Hiram and Maryette Thompson originally homesteaded the land. Their son Jimmy was born on the ranch in 1907. The local post office was located at the ranch. The original homestead cabin, log barn, and well all remain in use today. (Courtesy of Sprucedale Ranch.)

A horse rears while being worked at the Sprucedale Ranch. Ernest and Bertha Patterson bought the ranch in 1921. Shortly after, some cold, wet fishermen asked for a place to stay. The Pattersons cleaned out a storage shed for the men. As they left, the fishermen asked if they could return the following year. Ernest, a carpenter, built cabins and offered riding, and by 1922, the dude ranch was in business. (Courtesy of Sprucedale Ranch.)

Ernest's health started to deteriorate in the late 1930s. The Pattersons sold the ranch to friends and neighbors the Wiltbanks, pictured here in 1941. From left to right are Walt and Fay Wiltbank, Dorothy Hawes, Abe Malone, Margine ?, and Bud ? (Courtesy of Sprucedale Ranch.)

Walt is shown getting a ride organized at the Sprucedale Ranch. The Wiltbanks' early years were tough, made harder by the war. Walt farmed oats and barley, took guests riding, and used his packhorses to transport fishermen and their effects to the Black River, while Fay cooked and sold butter, eggs, and cheese at the CCC camp a few miles away. (Courtesy of Sprucedale Ranch.)

Emer Wiltbank, born in 1943, is seen feeding the chickens at the Sprucedale Ranch. Emer's parents, Walt and Fay, worked hard and found success and, over time, built seven more cabins. (Courtesy of Sprucedale Ranch.)

The Wiltbanks are pictured in front of the Sprucedale Ranch sign in 1965. From left to right are Emer, his wife, Esther, brother Ellis, Fay, and Walt. When Walt died in 1980, Fay asked Emer and Esther and their seven children—Fay, Billy, J.J., Stephanie, Emer, Whitney, and Tiffany—to keep the family traditions going. (Courtesy of Sprucedale Ranch.)

A morning ride takes place at Sprucedale Ranch in 1966. Some of the young colts are seen tagging along with their mothers. The Wiltbanks still raise and break most of their own horses. (Courtesy of Sprucedale Ranch.)

Children gather for a photograph on the woodpile at Sprucedale Ranch. Family is central to the operation, along with the authentic, traditional ranch experience that the Wiltbanks are known for. (Courtesy of Sprucedale Ranch.)

This is the main building at Sprucedale Ranch. Emer and Esther retired in 2004, and their son Whitney and his wife, Janae, took over the property. The third generation of Wiltbanks now hosts the third and fourth generations of guest families at Arizona's oldest operating dude ranch. (Courtesy of Sprucedale Ranch.)

Helen Zinsmeister poses with her horse at Circle Z Ranch in the 1920s. Helen and her husband, Lee, bought the 5,000-acre ranch from the Sanfords' daughter in 1925. The Sanfords had switched from cattle in 1881 and ran 13,000 sheep on the ranch until 1884. (Courtesy of Arizona Historical Society, BN23108.)

Above, Lee and Helen Zinsmeister water their horses in Sonoita Creek in the 1920s. Below, Lee Zinsmeister is pictured with a guest and a pet deer in the 1920s. In 1874, Denton Sanford of New York homesteaded what is now Circle Z Ranch. Several of Sanford's relatives also homesteaded in the area, eventually controlling 10 miles of the creek. Despite continued Apache raids, Sanford built a ranch, including a four-room adobe home. The ruins of the adobe building are still standing across the creek from the Circle Z complex. (Both, courtesy of Arizona Historical Society; above, BN2311; below, BN201402.)

Lee Zinsmeister is seen on horseback in front of Sanford Butte (Circle Z Mountain). The Zinsmeisters, from Germany, opened their new dude ranch near Patagonia in 1926, with a capacity of 26 guests. Over time, the ranch expanded to accommodate 70. (Courtesy of Circle Z Ranch.)

The interior of the adobe lodge at Circle Z Ranch is pictured here in the 1930s. In the early days, guests stayed an average of one month, with some staying the entire season. Private railcars owned by some guests were parked on a siding near the Patagonia station. (Courtesy of Circle Z Ranch.)

This photograph shows the traditional Fourth of July picnic at Circle Z Ranch. Beginning in 1929, the celebration hosted as many as 2,000 guests, who enjoyed pit barbecue, band concerts, a rodeo, and a dance. (Courtesy of Circle Z Ranch.)

Lee and Helen Zinsmeister are pictured with the Circle Z Ranch Cartuja Spanish stallion El Sultan and two of his colts. El Sultan was the only one of his breed in the United States. Established in the 15th century by Carthusian monks, the breed is known for its beauty and gentle disposition. To this day, Circle Z is noted for its fine horses, most of which are bred, raised, and trained on the ranch. (Courtesy of Circle Z Ranch.)

This was the first pool at Circle Z Ranch. All that is left today is the pipe that brought the water from Sonoita Creek and a depression in the ground near the horses' night pasture. (Courtesy of Circle Z Ranch.)

The original lodge building is shown here with Sanford Butte behind. This lodge burned to the ground in 1952 and was replaced by the Zinsmeister home. Following some short-term owners during the war years, Fred Fendig of Chicago bought the ranch in 1949 and ran it for 25 years. (Courtesy of Circle Z Ranch.)

Guests play polo at Circle Z Ranch. The ranch field was located on flatland under Sanford Butte and west of the corrals. The ranch has also been used often for movies and television shows, including *Broken Lance, Last Train from Gun Hill, Gunman's Walk, Devil's Angels, Monte Walsh, The Young Riders, Gunsmoke, Desperado,* and *Young Pioneers.* (Courtesy of Circle Z Ranch.)

Here is the 1937 trophy for best dude ranch entry in the Tucson Rodeo Parade. Preston and Lucia Nash purchased the Circle Z Ranch in 1974, with the express goal of continuing the ranch's honored traditions and protecting the land. Lucia's interest stemmed from her childhood visits with her family during the Zinsmeister years. (Courtesy of Arizona Historical Society, BN201399.)

This 1920s photograph shows a guest room at Circle Z Ranch. Throughout its long history (one of the longest in Arizona), Circle Z has been an active, well-known, and respected dude ranch. Lucia's son Rick and his wife, Diana, continue the tradition with 40-year ranch veteran George Lorta and his wife, Jennie. (Courtesy of Arizona Historical Society, BN201407.)

Guests take a break at the Y Lightning Ranch. This 25,000-acre working cattle ranch, named for its brand, was situated at a 4,800-foot elevation outside of Hereford. Operated from 1925 to 1961, the ranch offered hunting trips and visits to Naco and Agua Prieta, Mexico. (Courtesy of Arizona Historical Society, BN201477.)

This 1934 photograph shows riders in front of the Triangle T Ranch, located in Texas Canyon near Dragoon. Chiricahua Apache chief Cochise and his band used the ranch as a winter camp. The property was homesteaded in the early 1900s. Metta Tutt acquired it and opened a dude ranch in 1928. The ranch is named after her—*T* for Tutt. (Courtesy of Pomona Public Library.)

The living room at Triangle T Ranch is pictured here in 1934. The ranch has a varied history, which includes serving as the internment camp for the Japanese ambassador and 37 of his entourage during World War II. The ranch guest and reference lists include the names of Rockefellers and Vanderbilts. (Courtesy of Pomona Public Library.)

This is a 1934 view from above Triangle T Ranch. The wealthy, connected Tutts drew famous guests, including Pres. John F. Kennedy, Gen. John J. Pershing, Clarke Gable, Gregory Peck, Walt Disney, and the Lone Ranger (actor Clayton Moore). More recently, Steve McQueen and his brother Jodie, Johnny Cash, Willie Nelson, and Kris Kristofferson have been guests. (Courtesy of Pomona Public Library.)

Triangle T Ranch riders are pictured here among the boulders of Texas Canyon. This unique terrain has been featured in movies and television, including the original *3:10 to Yuma*, *Duel in the Sun*, *Tombstone*, *Geronimo*, *Along Came Jones*, and several Tom Mix films. *High Chaparral* was often filmed there, along with several more recent shows. The ranch remains open and continues to offer a beautiful location and fascinating history. (Courtesy of Triangle T Ranch.)

The dining and sitting rooms at Saguaro Lake Ranch are shown in these 1950s photographs. The ranch was originally the construction camp for workers building Stewart Mountain Dam between 1928 and 1930. Phil and Marie Lewis purchased the camp from the Salt River Project in 1930. Some of the buildings were moved and remodeled. Mexican artisans added native rock walls, porches, and fireplaces. Originally, the Lewis family operated the property as a fishing camp, general store, gas station, restaurant, and rental cabins. (Both, courtesy of Saguaro Lake Ranch.)

This is a busy corral scene at Saguaro Lake Ranch. During the 1930s, the Lewis family built the horse trails that surround the ranch. Rides traveled into the Goldfield Mountains, climbed the Bulldog Cliffs that overlook the ranch, and went into the washes and canyons around the ranch. (Courtesy of Saguaro Lake Ranch.)

Corrine Strowe points the way to Saguaro Lake Ranch in this 1940 photograph. (Courtesy of Saguaro Lake Ranch.)

Above, John Kissinger and Dorothy Durand pose beside their ranch sign. Below, Dorothy (right) is pictured with original partners Emory and Jean Hatch at Saguaro Lake Ranch. The partnership bought the ranch in 1948, with Dorothy becoming the sole owner by 1952. The ranch is located along the bank of the Salt River within the Tonto National Forest, just a short walk to Saguaro Lake. (Both, courtesy of Saguaro Lake Ranch.)

John Kissinger (Dorothy's husband) does a rope trick in this 1955 photograph. John was a "real cowboy" from Idaho who had worked at several dude ranches in Wyoming and Colorado. He also worked for Gene Autry. (Courtesy of Saguaro Lake Ranch.)

Below, a group is seen square dancing at Saguaro Lake Ranch. From 1948 to 1978, Dorothy Durand and John Kissinger ran the ranch. Then Dorothy's son Steve and his wife, Susan, took over the property. Their eldest son, Justin, is planning on being the next generation of Durands to operate the family ranch. (Courtesy of Saguaro Lake Ranch.)

Typical Guest House 76 Ranch   WILCOX ARIZONA   J-30

This postcard image shows a guest cottage at the 76 Ranch near Bonita. Still a cattle ranch, the 76 was established in the 1870s. It was the site of the Battle of KH Butte between the 6th Cavalry and the Apache Indians in 1881. Rumor has it that the ranch was founded on funds stolen in the Wham Paymaster Robbery of 1889. The 76 Ranch was a dude ranch from 1932 to 1955. (Author's collection.)

This view of a gate at Rancho Santa Cruz was used in a brochure for the property. The ranch is situated within the boundaries of the Spanish land grant Baca Float. The ranch is also a neighbor to Tumacacori, a Father Kino mission founded in 1691. (Author's collection.)

The wranglers are pictured with their horses at the Wrangler's Roost Ranch near New River. Originally, the ranch was a stage stop in the late 1800s. In 1930, Carl "Chief" Myers built a dude ranch that operated from 1935 through 1948. The ranch was reopened and operated from 1960 to 1972. (Author's collection.)

William Allen founded the Kenyon Ranch in 1937. Pictured here is one of the guest cabins. Allen and a few of his friends constructed the buildings out of stone. He had come from Ohio to vacation at the Circle Z Ranch near Patagonia. Finding the dry climate good for his asthma, Allen bought land and opened his dude ranch in 1938. The ranch was named for his alma mater, Kenyon College. (Courtesy of Arizona Historical Society, PC178f2HS93395.)

One of the living rooms at Kenyon Ranch is pictured here in the 1930s. Originally 100 acres, Kenyon Ranch was situated outside of Tubac at the foothills of the Tumacacori Mountains. William Allen and his wife, Marcella "Sis," expanded their ranch to 1,700 acres. From 1938 to 1973, Kenyon Ranch was one of the most active and successful ranches in Arizona. (Courtesy of Pomona Public Library.)

Here is a buckskin horse at Kenyan Ranch. The ranch was a destination for celebrities, including Cary Grant and Ricky Nelson. (Courtesy of Arizona Historical Society, PC178HS93499.)

Dudes are pictured here at Kenyon Ranch. Bill Allen, who served as president of the Southern Arizona Dude Ranch Association for two terms in the mid-1940s, died in 1962. His wife, Sis, and their daughter-in-law, Ann Nichols, ran the ranch for 11 more years. (Courtesy of Arizona Historical Society, PC178HS93471.)

Young dudes (often called "dudettes" in the early days) clean the dishes at Kenyan Ranch. The Allen family sold the ranch in 1973. Charles and Barbara Findeisen bought the property in 2003. It is currently operated as a retreat center, hosting events, workshops, reunions, and so on. Guests who knew the ranch in its heyday say the magic is still there. (Courtesy of Arizona Historical Society, PC178f2HS93498.)

Rancho Grande guests wave to the camera in this 1940 photograph. A group of civic-minded citizens from the Nogales area built Rancho Grande in 1927. Originally called Hotel Esplendor, the ranch closed for several years because of the Depression, then reopened in 1938. (Courtesy of Pomona Public Library.)

This 1940 photograph shows the size and style of the Rancho Grande located on a hill three miles north of the border outside of Nogales. In late 1941, Lynn Gillham, well known as owner/operator of Tucson's Flying V Ranch, took over management. (Courtesy of Pomona Public Library.)

The rolling hills of the border country serve as a backdrop for this 1940 photograph of a corral at Rancho Grande. The ranch offered extensive hunting, but riding was the focus. In 1951, the ranch scheduled two rodeos and issued a challenge to Tucson cowboys—to come south and compete against Nogales cowboys. (Courtesy of Pomona Public Library.)

The impressive Southwest-style living room at Rancho Grande is pictured here in 1940. A 1946 advertisement in Tucson announces round-trip flights (Tucson/Nogales) on DC-3s of Arizona Airways for $18, including a room and meals for two nights. Sometime in the early 1950s, the ranch went back to operating as a hotel. Eventually, it burned down. (Courtesy of Pomona Public Library.)

This postcard shows a view of the front lawn at the Cochise Lodge and Guest Ranch, located outside of Elfrida. From 1947 to 1956, the ranch was called the EM–Bar–Bee. In 1957, the ranch briefly took on the name of Swisshelm Lodge and Guest Ranch after the nearby mountains. In 1958, the television show *Sheriff of Cochise* ran a nationwide contest for a vacation at the Cochise Lodge. The ranch closed in 1977 when owners Charles and Mildred Thumm were murdered. (Author's collection.)

This postcard image shows a ride coming through the Rex Ranch, near Amado. The 50-acre ranch was a part of the 1820 Ignacio de la Canoa Mexican land grant. One of the ranch buildings was constructed in the late 1880s by a cavalry officer who was given the property upon his retirement. The first official building permit was issued in 1936. (Author's collection.)

Another postcard depicts a two-story adobe guest accommodation designed by Josiah Joessler in the 1950s. In 1938, Rex Hamaker of Houston purchased the ranch and sometime later, after enlarging and remodeling the property, opened it as a dude ranch. Rex Ranch operated into the 1980s. (Author's collection.)

Shown here is the original home at the Trappman Ranch that Herman and Mary homesteaded in 1880 and ranched until their deaths. Stone and concrete cisterns, a rock-lined, hand-dug well, and some adobe walls remain a part of what is now Tombstone Monument Ranch. (Courtesy Tombstone Monument Ranch.)

The Schieffelin Monument is seen in the background of this Tombstone Monument Ranch photograph. Ed Schieffelin, the founder of Tombstone, had asked in his will that he be buried beneath a prospector's monument in the rocks where he successfully hid out from a band of Apaches searching for him. (Courtesy of Laura True.)

The Tombstone Monument Ranch is seen in this photograph. Between the Trappman ranch and the town of Tombstone were Ernest Escapule's YC Bar and K Open A Ranches. In 1946, Ernest sold the ranches to Lee Zinsmeister, who by that time had sold the Circle Z Ranch. His wife, Helen, renamed the combined ranches the Lucky Hills Ranch. (Courtesy of Laura True.)

This is the 1800s-style bar at Tombstone Monument Ranch. The dude ranch was built on the historic Escapule Ranch (Trappman descendents) in 2009. The multigenerational Escapule family remains an important part of Tombstone. Still visible beneath the bar is the original ranch root cellar and tunnel for escape from Apache Indian attacks. (Courtesy of Laura True.)

The main building of the Fresnal Ranch School (now Elkhorn Ranch) is pictured with Fresnal Peak in the background. Founded in 1929, the school located in the Baboquivari Mountains maintained a working cattle ranch where the students worked one day per week. Each boy had his own horse. The school closed in 1942 because of World War II. (Courtesy of Elkhorn Ranch Archives.)

Ernest and Grace Miller and their son Bob are framed by a tree in this 1940s photograph taken at Elkhorn Ranch. The Millers got into the dude ranch business in 1922 when Ernie bought a cabin that had been damaged by bears near Bozeman, Montana, for $500. That summer, four guests stayed in the cabin while Ernie and Grace slept outside under a tree. They steadily added land and built cabins, creating the Montana Elkhorn Ranch. (Courtesy of Elkhorn Ranch Archives.)

Bob and Jan Miller are pictured with their daughter Linda in 1954. Bob's father, Ernie, had traveled through Tucson to Mexico when guiding hunting trips. The Millers started looking in the area, and Jim Converse, founder of Tanque Verde Ranch, helped them find the closed Fresnal Ranch School. Elkhorn Ranch South opened in 1946. (Courtesy of Elkhorn Ranch Archives.)

In this view, Grace Miller is seen behind the radio, and Jan Miller is seated on the chaise at right. During the 1940s and 1950s, guests of Elkhorn Ranch gathered on Saturdays to listen to the Texaco broadcast of the Metropolitan Opera. Bridget, the ranch burro, often wandered over to add braying to an aria. (Courtesy of Elkhorn Ranch Archives.)

Three generations of Millers are shown in this photograph. From left to right are (first row) Mary, Alicia, Jan, and Clara; (second row) Tom, Charley, and Bob. In 1961, Bob and Jan took over complete management of Elkhorn Ranch South, and the seasonal treks ended. (Courtesy of Elkhorn Ranch.)

This iconic photograph from the early 1950s shows Bob Miller and Ellie Kronfeld Andrews perched high up in Elkhorn Ranch country. Unlike so many other ranches affected by development, the Elkhorn views remain largely unchanged. (Courtesy of Elkhorn Ranch Archives.)

Charley Miller is seen training a horse in this photograph. The Millers of Elkhorn Ranch raise many of their own horses, combining Percheron, Thoroughbred, and Quarter Horse blood to make strong, sturdy horses with good minds. Charley closely manages his own riding program as well. Charley and Mary Miller are award-winning stewards of their land and continue to consistently honor the traditions started by the first generation of their family. (Courtesy of Heather Dawe, YDuckie Imaging.)

INDEX